THE BARMAN

Helen Bowell is a poet, critic .... She is a co-director of Dead [Women] Poets Society, a live literature organisation which 'resurrects' women poets of the past. Helen is a Ledbury Poetry Critic and an alumna of The Writing Squad, Roundhouse Poetry Collective, London Writers Awards and London Library Emerging Writers Programme. Her work has appeared in *Magma*, *The North*, *Poetry Wales*, *Ambit*, *harana poetry* and elsewhere. Since 2017, she has worked at The Poetry Society.

The Barman

Published by Bad Betty Press in 2022
www.badbettypress.com

Helen Bowell has asserted her right to be identified as the author of this work in accordance with Section 77 of the Copyright, Designs and Patents Act of 1988.

Cover illustration by Anita Marante

Printed and bound in the United Kingdom

A CIP record of this book is available from the British Library.

ISBN: 978-1-913268-25-1

Supported using public funding by
ARTS COUNCIL ENGLAND

LOTTERY FUNDED

THE
BARMAN

PRESS

Contents

Lobster

Here's one from near the end:
the barman's cooking with no music on,
no wine, no candles, and the knives are blunt,
he slips and nips himself chopping onion –
Fuck!

I told him the most dangerous item
in the kitchen is a blunt knife but
I sit on the sofa,
not letting the news in,
the TV offering

Gardeners' World,
The Chase, Friends,
and I know that statistically
right now someone's watching Rachel
get off the plane.

I want to ask what they'd do
in her nice shoes –
it's just not a good look
to stunt your career
for some jealous guy

who lied about divorcing you,
dated his student,
called another your name
at the altar – maybe that one's okay –
still –

and the barman, who's done none of these things,
is fumbling with the onions, his finger gushing,
and something clunks to the floor –
Fuck! Fucking –
fuck!

and I think about the knife-sharpener in the top drawer
and I think about how I want my life to be
and answering Bradley Walsh's question
about Edvard Munch, *The Scream*,
I say out loud, *The Scream*.

Barman in Eden

In the autumn, the barman and I visit Eden.
They have put up signs since the last time I was here.

Some say DO NOT WALK ON THE GRASS;
others inform guests about the mass extinction.

A dragonfly bumps into a leaf. A peregrine
falcon nose-dives. A mother asks us for money.

I want to change everything
and nothing. The barman takes my hand,

suggests a tea break. I buy a fresh scone,
the exact shape of the barman's fist.

In the gift shop, we touch everything:
HOPE is printed in big letters on tea towels.

I know time is measured in Celsius.
At least I have enjoyed the seasons.

When we go home, even the sun
looks away.

If You Can Go to Hell for Lust

after Hieronymus Bosch

Can I give you this trout for safe-keeping?
Don't look like that, with your hand on my wrist.
I am an owl staring at what I've done.
Will you hide with me in this tight red cone?
Will you carry me on your back when I'm trapped in a clam?
Take me into the trees.
Place a ball in my mouth with your beak.
I am facing the biggest fish of my life.
Put a toad on my chest and touch me.
Put me in a drum and bang me.
Look at that man, skating on ice.
Oh, barman, I'm trying to make this boat go
but I just don't know how.

The Moderating Influence of the Sea

This elbow-crook of the island
has its own microclimate.

Many plants are considered
too tender to survive.

I like reading the signs.
The barman prefers to keep moving.

I want to take his hand
but I'll get clammy.

I worry people think
I'm a tourist, even when I am one.

The barman casts a shadow.
I hate that I burn in the sun.

At least the sea is warmer here
than in the rest of this frost-land.

I take my clothes off.
The barman waits on the sand.

He didn't bring his trunks,
though he knows how I love to swim.

I Know He'd Never Really Say This But

I had a dream the barman couldn't find his favourite pen
and called me a slanty-eyed thief.
He pulled at the corners of his eyes
like the boys in primary school.

I told him I hadn't touched it.
I said, Have you checked the bedside table?
He grew the length of a ruler.
He told me to go back home.

In the dream, I didn't demand an apology.
I don't know if dream-me took the dream-pen
and, if so, why. Sometimes the hardest questions
are the ones you ask yourself. I asked him to forgive me.

Small

I'm so good at squashing all my feelings
into the perfect toastie – pricey cheese,
fresh tomatoes – these days
I don't even feel them going down.

It's good to save space
for the barman's feelings,
which he can't swallow, or name,
but leak from him like chip grease.

And I love chips. I'd lick
the newspaper clean, if I had to.

The Barwoman

One night I ask the barman if he's ever thought about other men like that. Like what? He's flicking through the channels, going panel show/ talent show/Daniel Craig running on buses again. Like, in a sexy way. He laughs. No.

All I want is for him to ask me back. Instead, he says, I'm knackered. Think I'll head up to bed.

Fighting the Barman

I want to say the barman and I fight
all the time. I want to say he'd stake

his life on the noughties' best
boy band, that he wouldn't speak to me

for two days when I suggested Emma
Watson was boring. Or that

he got so upset when he thought
I didn't sort my rubbish

that he ignored me when I asked
if he took milk in his tea. I wish

I could tell you how he ranted
for a whole episode of *Fleabag*

about why I should vote tactically
and not Green, before I yelled I'd vote

for Boris if it meant I could Get This
Conversation Done. I want

to tell you about the *sorry* after,
how we each tried to prove ourselves

the better lover. That there were eggs
in the morning, a Reece's cup

on the counter. I want to say our love
feels like lifting weights, but it's like

doing five minutes of yoga and hoping
for the best, like ten rounds of chin-ups

when your feet never leave the ground.
I want to say we could rebuild this house

if all we had left were the nine drunk selfies
we snapped early on, outside the pub

after last orders, our teeth still
white and hard as promises.

Scaredy Barman

The barman pretended to be scared of spiders,
when really he was just being lazy. I had to down

my cup of water and cage it when he screamed.
It was huge! It was fucking huge!

I'm only scared when I'm on my own, picturing
their long legs creeping between my sleeping lips.

One time a man spray-painted WHORE
on my friend's house while she slept.

I would have taken him out like that spider,
scooped him up with the biggest cup

and a letter from the council, if I'd been there.
But he scuttled away. And though he could scuttle

back at any moment, I've never been a spider-killer.
I just can't bring myself to squash them.

Cheer

I'm a cheerleader in the upcoming game. Pom one, pom two. Rattle like snakes. I ask the squad about the routine and they say Just keep smiling. Look, I know I don't have the hair for the gig, or the shoes. But does that matter? Sometimes the barman comes to watch. Sometimes my parents, or old friends. I know I can pull off the red: I have the right genes. Anyway, all women look good in white. I am a glass Coke bottle standing on the shoulders of glass Coke bottles, waiting to be knocked. Some nights the cheers hurt my ears. The game gets violent. Someone hurts someone else. My job is not to reflect the world as it is, but as we all want it to look. Give me a B, give me an A, give me an R.

Barman on Tour (II)

The barman and I go to China on holiday. Things are getting serious but not so serious that I tell my very distant family we're there.

For the first time in his life, the barman is getting stared at in the street. Two men ask for a selfie with him and the Bird's Nest Stadium. On the underground, teens in school uniforms openly point and laugh. He's never felt so handsome and strange. When we kiss, I can feel him smiling, light as a blimp.

The morning I venture out for breakfast alone, a shopkeeper stops me to say I'm beautiful. I guess from her smile and my little Chinese that she's saying I'm mixed.

Back at the hotel, I relay this to the barman and he chuckles. Arm round me, he says, I think you're beautiful too, and switches on the TV.

If I Were an AI Would the Barman Tell Me?

Sometimes people stare
like I have shiny giveaway skin,
and my joints harden in the cold,
and all I want to do
is stop the terrible electronic
photo album of my brain
and think about
my lovely boyfriend
like a normal person

but other times
I'm secretly pleased
I'm not like the barman
and his people.
I mean, look at them.
They traipse mud
through the house
and don't know how
to eat lo mai gai.
We give the biggest morsels
to the ones we love

and I don't know
if I love the barman
enough to tell
him the truth.

Summer

We laze before the telly and through the windows
the great flash photographer in the sky does their work.

It is easy to say I love you now.
He nuzzles me with his head,

hair still wet, the froth on a pint of bitter.
A hint of day in the yellow clouds.

Chicken

Here's one from the middle:
barman hungry, Deliveroo on strike
so he opens the new Dishoom book
and makes his own damn chicken ruby.
It tastes so good we vow never
to order over-priced grease again
till we spend the night not touching,
taking (bad) turns in the toilet
and, once, in the sink.
In the morning, the barman turns
to me sweat-faced and sorry
and says, I've ordered new sheets
and a friend is dropping off
some Lucozade and bread,
and I could – but don't – kiss
his sweet salty forehead,
still gleaming with cumin.

Together We'll Meet in Downward-Facing Dog

for Meri

The barman and I are learning about our bodies.
We are opening our hips, though we're scared

of what might happen. After this, coffee, porridge, work.
It's too easy to push away from the earth, to say

Namaste with our hands pressed to our temples.
Adriene says, Find what feels good. I worry

I'll never be strong enough to lift my body up safely,
but Adriene says Get on all fours, so we do.

What feels good? Sometimes I don't know.
I hoover every spot of the living room.

Open Your Mouth and See What Happens

I admit it. I put sixteen books by my bedside for show. My cheese plant is dead. What if the barman is only joking? Pass. What if I'm going to be alone forever? Pass. I am sitting on a bar stool, trying not to cry.

Money

The crowds are chanting again.
Of course they are.

The bad guys are killing people
with guns, rockets, knees,

stones, camps, hands,
and they're getting really good at golf.

I butter toast this side of the ocean,
signing petitions between gulps of tea,

telling the barman to spend
money where we should.

Every life depends on misery
being elsewhere, and I'm sick

of the union jacks so I write
to my MP who agrees with me,

I donate to small charities,
I talk and talk and talk,

and the barman listens,
a red post box

with his mouth wide open,
waiting for better news.

The Barman Puts the Kettle On

Sugar? asks the barman, or are you too sweet?
I think, Don't call me sugar, and say,
Sweet enough, it's supposed to be.
I'm flat on the barman's bed. He hands me
my tea and I sip but it's too hot, too white.
These things take time. I want to know: what
sandwich would he be? What Disney princess?
I only know the names of two of his friends –
both men – and he hasn't asked where
I'm really from yet. I know his favourite
uncle's in the police, and haven't broken
the news to my housemates. It's too hot.
The barman opens a window. Sirens.
How much longer will this go on?

Monsieur le Barman

The barman is learning French. I already speak French and he knows how I love to tell people what they're doing wrong. His accent is particularly awful but you really have to live somewhere to pick that kind of thing up.

It's Tuesday night and the pub's empty. The barman sprays half a pint of Sprite into a glass and asks what *remember* is in French.

Se souvenir de, I say. It's reflexive. And irregular, like venir.

Too complicated for me, he says, opening a pack of cheese and onion crisps.

Je parle français et pas cantonais.

Ma grand-mère ne savait parler que cantonais.

佢歸西.

I want to say all this to the barman, but I think it would be too much. So instead, we do verb drills: je suis, tu es, il/elle/on est. Et c'est facile.

Front Crawl

after Emily Berry

I go swimming with the barman.
I consider not wearing goggles
so as to appear more sensual and less
like a frog, but I can't take the chlorine.

I have to do lengths. Just a few.
Even if the barman minds,
he'll get used to it.
He assures me he's fine,

but I keep looking back
down the lane to check.
He nearly drowned
when he was fifteen,

the river too fast, the ciders
too quick. His friend dove in,
kick-boxed the current,
and the water let him go.

He says luck didn't come
into it, it wasn't so bad,
he could have swum out of it.
And suddenly I can't see him –

I stop mid-lane,
splash to the side and hoist
my slimy self out
to find him laughing. Good joke.

I slide back in and do my very best
breast-stroke, thinking how
the barman couldn't say
what luck was to save his life.

Barman on Tour (I)

When I stumble upstairs on the bus,
the barman is sitting in my favourite seat.

He says, Fancy seeing you here. I say,
Fancy indeed. He pats the blue pile beside him

and I oblige. Where are you headed?
I ask. The barman looks out the window

as if the traffic holds great interest.
Southend-on-Sea. It is not possible

to get to Southend-on-Sea by bus
from Charing Cross but I don't question it.

The barman opens a bag of Smarties
and offers me a handful. I've stopped buying

them since I found out about Nestlé,
but because it's him, and because

where we're going I might need the fuel,
and because it's so hot the sugar shells

are melting in his thick fingers like warm balls
of earwax, yes, okay, I accept, I accept.

The Barman's Eyesight

The barman's glasses are horn-rimmed,
tortoise shell, the perfect animal/human combo.
He wears them as close to the bridge of his nose as he can.
His mother once said he looked better with them on.
The barman is always wiping his glasses
on his beer-battered t-shirts. Really,
the glasses clean the clothes.
Towards the end of one shift, the barman
removes his spectacles and rubs his eyes
with his palms. What's wrong? I ask.

What isn't? He folds up the papers,
cleans the counter, takes an order,
cuts into a butter-soft avocado.
He's going to smash it, in this pub
in the middle of austerity, serve it
on sourdough drenched in olive oil
from Cyprus. It's so delicious
I could scream. He knows as well as I do
how much this all costs, but we say nothing,
and the lights flicker like eyes struggling not to shut.

Back Story

So I made myself a seagull
dyed everything grey and white
glued sexless feathers to a Weetabix box
and circled the school carpark

bombing children with lip-shaped
sweets if I liked them
and smaller creatures' eggs
if I didn't

hovered by the gates studying
how girls in bunches became bananas
still green and hard
but not as hard as me

I was an unblinking seagull
always out of reach
I was the chip-stealer
the sky-klaxon

a squawk so loud
nobody would want
to hurt me
couldn't if they tried

and I beat my wings
till the white vans and boys
in their bad uniforms
blew out out out to sea

Scrabble

Here's a story from the start: barman cleaning up,
most people gone or hysterically laughing, I say,
What's your name anyway? He says, Don't you know?
I know yours. I say, How? He says, You told me.
I say, I was very drunk. He says, Yes,
and that Scrabble move really shouldn't
have counted. I say, what – spaghetti?
That's a great move! He says, not spelt
S P A G E T E E, it's not.
I should have known then
the barman could never let anything go.

Acknowledgements

Thank you to the publications and organisations who have published versions of these poems: *bath magg*, Creative Future, *Mslexia*, Verve Poetry Festival and Winchester Poetry Festival.

Thank you to all the people and organisations who've supported my work over the last decade, including Steve Dearden and all the poets at The Writing Squad; Cecilia Knapp, Bridget Minamore and all my Roundhouse Poetry Collective cohort; Julia Bird, Jenny Danes, Jamie Hale, Annie Hayter and Lisa Kiew who helped me edit many of these poems; and Jacqueline Saphra in whose Poetry School workshop I started writing barman poems (unbeknownst to her), and who commended 'Monsieur le Barman' in the Winchester Poetry Competition 2021.

Thank you to Amy Acre and Jake Wild Hall at Bad Betty Press and to my generous editor Gboyega Odubanjo for believing in this work.

Thank you to my parents, all my family and my friends for their endless love and support, and to Anita Marante for the cover art and everything else.

Lightning Source UK Ltd.
Milton Keynes UK
UKHW010223210122
397500UK00001B/35